MILITARY HELICOPTERS

HEROES OF THE SKY

Taylor Baldwin Kiland and Karen and Glen Bledsoe

Published in 2016 by Enslow Publishing, LLC.
101 W. 23rd Street, Suite 240, New York, NY 10011

Library of Congress Cataloging-in-Publication Data

Kiland, Taylor Baldwin, 1966–
   Military helicopters : heroes of the sky / Taylor Baldwin Kiland and Karen and Glen Bledsoe.
       pages cm. —(Military engineering in action)
   Includes bibliographical references and index.
   Summary: "Describes the development, use, and abilities of helicopters in the military"—Provided by publisher.
   Audience: Grades 7-8.
   ISBN 978-0-7660-6912-1 (library binding)
   ISBN 978-0-7660-7063-9 (pbk.)
   ISBN 978-0-7660-7064-6 (6-pack)
   1. Military helicopters—United States—Juvenile literature. 2. Helicopter pilots—United States—Juvenile literature. I. Bledsoe,
   Glen. II. Title.
   UG1233.K55 2015
   358.4'183—dc23
                              2015011218

Printed in the United States of America

To Our Readers: We have done our best to make sure all Web site addresses in this book were active and appropriate when we went to press. However, the author and the publisher have no control over and assume no liability for the material available on those Web sites or on any Web sites they may link to. Any comments or suggestions can be sent by e-mail to customerservice@enslow.com.

Portions of this book originally appeared in *Helicopters: HIgh-Flying Heroes.*

Photo Credits: A Periam Photography/Shutterstock.com, p. 45; © AP Images, pp. 15, 16, 28, 29, 43; courtesy of DVIDS, p. 26; Dennis Steen/Shutterstock.com, p. 37; iralu/Shutterstock.com, p. 11; Sascha Hahn/Shutterstock.com, pp. 2, 4; Shutterstock.com (art/backgrounds throughout book): Dianka Pyzhova, Ensuper, foxie, kasha_malasha, pashabo; Sgt. 1st Class Eric Pahon/DVIDS, p. 25; Tech Sgt. Matt Hecht/DVIDS, p. 32; US Air National Guard photo/Maj. Dale Greer, p. 31; US Army photo, pp. 13, 21; US Army/Wikimedia Commons/Sikorsky S-55 inflight c.jpg/Public Domain, p. 47; US Army photo by Barbara Romano, p. 1 (soldiers, right); US Army photo by 1st Lt. Benjamin J. Postle, p. 35; US Army photo by 1st Lt. Katherine Kaliski, 166th Aviation Brigade, Division West, Public Affairs, p. 19; US Army photo by Sgt. Michael J. MacLeod, p. 40; US Army photo by Spc. Bryanna Poulin, p. 1 (helicopter, left); US Army National Guard photo by Staff Sgt. Brendan Mackie, p. 44; US Coast Guard photo by Petty Officer 2nd Class NyxoLyno Cangemi, p. 9; US Navy photo by Chief Photographer's Mate Johnny Bivera, p. 18; US Navy photo by Mass Communication Specialist 1st Class Jon Rasmussen, p. 23; US Navy photo by Mass Communication Specialist 3rd Class Kegan E. Kay, p. 24; US Navy photo by Photographers Mate 2nd Class Michael Sandberg, p. 41; US Navy photo by Photographer's Mate 3rd Class Shawn Hussong, p. 8; US Navy photo by Photographer's Mate 3rd Class Timothy Bensken, p. 7; Stocktreck Images/Getty Images, pp. 36, 38.

Cover Credits: US Army photo by Barbara Romano (soldiers, front right); US Army photo by Spc. Bryanna Poulin (helicopter, front left); SAC Tim Laurence/© Crown Copyright 2013/Open Government Licence (helicopter, back); Shutterstock.com: kasha_malasha (camouflage background), foxie (series logo).

CONTENTS

Three military helicopters fly in formation.

CHAPTER 1

Speed and Agility in the Combat Zone

It was a complicated mission in the middle of a fierce battle. Civil war was raging in North Africa, and US Marines assigned to the Medium Tiltrotor Squadron 266 were mobilized to fly 150 miles (241 kilometers) at night. Their mission: to rescue an air force F-15E pilot whose plane crashed near Benghazi, Libya, in March 2011. Known as the First Battle of Benghazi, this conflict pitted army units loyal to Libya's then-leader Muammar Gaddafi against anti-Gaddafi forces.

Marine Captain Erik Kolle and his two crew chiefs, Staff Sergeant David Potter and Sergeant Daniel Howington, took off from the amphibious assault ship USS *Kearsarge*. They arrived on the scene in their V-22 Osprey helicopter in less than ninety minutes and rescued the pilot, who was running for his life to evade capture by the enemy. No other helicopter or transport vehicle beside this V-22 Osprey could have performed such a mission.

The unusual aircraft, which takes off and lands like a helicopter, can rotate its engines to fly forward like a regular airplane. The chopper has been operational only since 2007, but it has become a favorite for all kinds of missions, including freight transport and medical transport. It is also the perfect vehicle for enemy assaults, where it carries loads of Marines into and out of combat landing zones. Twice as fast as its predecessor, the CH-46 Sea Knight, the V-22 Osprey has a longer range and can carry more cargo and more than twice as many troops.

In an interview in January 2013, Captain Kolle said, "I'm not going to say that a V-22 is required for every TRAP [tactical recovery of aircraft and personnel mission], but for this one it was. There were some other helicopter assets in the Mediterranean at the time, but because of the distances involved they either wouldn't have had enough gas or would have taken several hours longer." Captain Kolle, Staff Sergeant Potter, and Sergeant Howington were awarded the Air Medal with the Combat Distinguishing Device for Valor for their successful mission that night.

Different Types and Different Missions

The V-22 Osprey is just one kind of military helicopter. Helicopters are used by all branches of the military for combat missions and for rescue. Attack helicopters are armed with high-powered weapons such as machine guns and missiles (rockets carrying explosives that may be launched by remote control). These weapons are used in battle to attack targets on the ground. Large transport helicopters, like the Chinook, are used for moving soldiers and cargo from one place to another. They may move tanks and other military vehicles as well as large numbers of troops. Smaller transport helicopters are used to move weapons, food, medical equipment, and smaller numbers of troops. They may also rescue downed jet pilots or troops who are trapped by opposing forces.

A US Marine Corps V-22 Osprey, an advanced technology, vertical/short takeoff and landing multipurpose tactical aircraft, takes off vertically from the flight deck of the USS *Wasp*.

Different branches of the military use different models of helicopters suited to the missions they perform. The army, navy, air force, and marines all use light transport, heavy transport, and attack helicopters, although each branch uses different models. The coast guard uses transport helicopters for search-and-rescue operations and for finding and stopping smugglers, or people trying to sneak goods into or out of the United States.

Military helicopters may also be used to rescue civilians, or nonmilitary citizens. The coast guard and the navy use helicopters to rescue boaters in distress. Army, air force, or National Guard helicopters may be called in to help rescue injured hikers or mountain climbers.

DART: *Downed Aircraft Recovery Team*

If something goes wrong on a military helicopter while flying in a war zone, the pilot may make an emergency landing wherever he or she can. Often it is far from any road and far from help. If the pilot cannot make the necessary repairs to get into the air again, a Downed Aircraft Recovery Team (DART) may be sent in to help.

A DART crew is usually made up of sixteen trained mechanics aboard a Chinook helicopter. When an emergency call comes in, the crew flies out to find the downed aircraft. Part of the crew makes quick repairs. Other crew members stand guard in case of attack. If the DART can get the helicopter in the air again, they will escort it back to an air base. If they cannot fix the helicopter, the crew may use their Chinook to carry it back to the base by "sling loading" the damaged vehicle. To do this, the DART crew places the downed aircraft onto a swing that is suspended from the Chinook helicopter and flown to a maintenance facility. At the base, larger repair crews will take over and fix the helicopter.

This DART crew is disembarking a CH-47 Chinook helicopter.

During natural disasters, helicopters may be used to help rescue people and move them away from the disaster zone. When Hurricane Katrina struck New Orleans in August 2005, the navy, the coast guard, and the National Guard responded immediately by sending in helicopters to rescue people who were trapped in the flooded city. Before the disaster was over, all branches of the military responded with helicopters and other rescue vehicles.

Flying over New Orleans in a HH-60J Jayhawk, a member of the coast guard looks for Hurricane Katrina survivors.

Parts of a Helicopter

Every model of helicopter differs from others. But all helicopters have certain parts in common.

MAIN ROTOR: The set of blades on the top of a helicopter. As they spin like the blades on an electric fan, they generate lift to help the helicopter rise into the air. All helicopters have at least one set of rotors. Some have two, stacked on top of each other, that spin in opposite directions. Some have two separate rotors, located one in front of the other. The main rotor is horizontal (parallel to the ground).

ENGINE: Sits at the top of a helicopter, just beneath the main rotor. It provides power to the helicopter, making the rotors spin and providing electricity for the various systems on board.

FRONT FUSELAGE: Part of the body of the aircraft that contains the cockpit, which is where the pilot sits and where the helicopter's controls are.

MAIN FUSELAGE: The space inside a helicopter where passengers or cargo may be carried. Also called the cabin.

TAIL BOOM: The part of the helicopter extending out behind the cabin, on which the tail rotor is mounted.

TAIL ROTOR: A vertical (perpendicular to the ground) rotor at the end of the tail boom. This rotor holds the helicopter's body straight in the air. The tail rotor can also help steer the aircraft by moving the tail boom.

SKIDS, FLOATS, OR WHEELS: The gear that supports the helicopter when it lands. The type of gear depends on the type of helicopter and where it is expected to land. Skids are useful on soft or uneven ground. Floats are for water landings. Wheels work well on solid ground, where the helicopter may have to move across the ground.

Basic Parts of a Helicopter

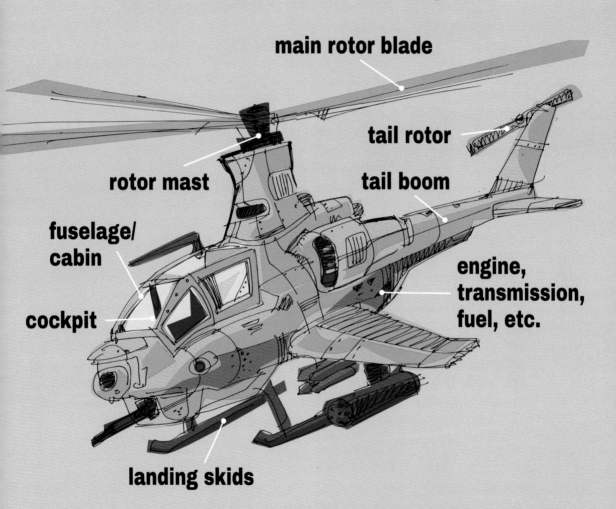

main rotor blade

tail rotor

rotor mast

tail boom

fuselage/
cabin

engine,
transmission,
fuel, etc.

cockpit

landing skids

The History of Planes That Hover

Inventors began experimenting with helicopter flight at the beginning of the twentieth century, but devising a plane that "hovers" proved harder to engineer than a fixed wing airplane. Designing a plane that took off and landed vertically, but flew horizontally, took many years to perfect. They were not used in military operations until several decades after the debut of the fixed wing airplane. In addition to their widespread military use, helicopters' commercial availability has had a profound impact on transportation and communications throughout the world.

Igor Sikorsky: The Father of Helicopters

The first helicopter that was actually able to fly was built by Raúl Pateras de Pescara of Argentina in 1916. In 1934, German engineers

A Chinook helicopter flies over International Security Assistance Forces as it prepares to drop soldiers off in Afghanistan.

built the first helicopter whose movement could be controlled by the pilot. These were only single models. No one was producing large numbers of helicopters. In the United States, Russian-born Igor Sikorsky would change that.

In 1939, Sikorsky built the VS-300, which lifted a few feet into the air and was fully controllable. Because of his success, Sikorsky sought out military contracts to build bigger and better helicopters. In 1943, he put a new model, the R-4, into production for military use.

The United States had been involved in World War II (1939–1945) since 1941. The Sikorsky R-4 helicopter proved useful in searching for submarines and looking for opposing troops. In 1945, helicopters lifted seventy wounded soldiers from a battle on Luzon, an island in the Philippines, to field hospitals. This was the first time that helicopters were used near a battle.

Helicopters were also used in the Korean War (1950–1953)—to transport wounded soldiers to field hospitals, to provide small supplies to remote combat units inaccessible by road, and for reconnaissance. The navy used them to pluck downed aviators from the sea and to undertake short logistical missions between ships. By then, other companies, such as Bell Aircraft, were building military helicopters. It was during this time that the helicopter got the nickname of "chopper," from the "chop-chop" sound made by the turning rotors.

The United States used military helicopters widely during the Vietnam War, from 1965 to 1973. In fact, this conflict has been frequently called "the Helicopter War," and many Vietnam combat veterans will say that the sound of an approaching helicopter brings back vivid memories of their wartime experiences. Thousands of helicopters were used to move troops into battle and to fly wounded soldiers to hospitals. Most of these were the Bell UH-1 helicopter, nicknamed the "Huey." Helicopters were also armed with machine guns so that they could fly over targets and fire at them. These were the first attack helicopters.

WORLDS RECORD
BROKEN
1 HOUR 20 MIN

Aviation pioneer Igor Sikorski flew the helicopter himself in 1941 to set a new record for time in the air.

The Korean War, September 1951, marks the first time that helicopters were used to carry troops to battle on an actual battlefront.

Today's Military Helicopters

Modern helicopters have many improvements over the first military helicopters. They use onboard navigation systems that help pilots find their way in the air. They carry radio equipment to communicate with other aircraft and with personnel on the ground. Many helicopters have radar warning systems that warn of approaching missiles.

Military helicopters may also carry weapons. The kind of weapons they carry depends on the type of helicopter. Transport helicopters are often armed with machine guns, which they use

How Helicopters Fly

A helicopter has at least one horizontal rotor that lifts it off the ground. It also has a second rotor, either horizontal or vertical, located on the tail, that keeps the craft from spinning with the rotor. The second rotor also helps steer the craft by moving the tail. Inside the cockpit, the pilot uses rudder pedals on the floor to control the tail movement.

Helicopters use some of the same principles of flight as airplanes do. Airplanes must move forward at high speeds to get enough air moving downward off the wings to generate lift. Lift is the force that raises an aircraft off the ground. A helicopter's rotor blades are shaped like long, thin wings. Rather than moving forward to generate lift, an engine turns the main rotor at high speed, forcing air downward. This allows helicopters to lift nearly straight off the ground. Because the helicopter needs no forward motion to generate lift, it can hover in one place.

Helicopters also move forward, backward, and to the side by slightly tilting the rotors. This allows the air coming off of the rotor to push both down and slightly backward, forward, or sideways. To do this, the pilot uses control sticks, or levers. The pilot also moves the levers to increase the angle of the rotor blades, allowing the helicopter to climb or descend.

mostly for defense. Attack helicopters carry machine guns but are also armed with missile launchers.

The size of a helicopter's crew depends on the helicopter. Large Chinook transport helicopters have a crew of three or more. The pilot and copilot fly the helicopter. The flight engineer checks the helicopter before and after each flight and keeps track of all systems during the flight. Chinooks may carry other crew members who assist with special missions.

Small transport helicopters usually have a crew of four, including a pilot, copilot, and one or more crew chiefs who carry out the work of the mission. They may also carry a gunner who controls and fires the weapons. Small attack helicopters usually carry a crew of only two: the pilot and the copilot.

US Marines on a mission in Afghanistan fly in a CH-46E Sea Knight helicopter.

Helicopters in the Sand

Every time a helicopter takes off or lands, the rotors kick up loose dust and dirt. But pilots landing helicopters in the deserts of the Middle East face a special challenge. In the desert, countless grains of loose sand can be whipped up by swirling helicopter rotors, forming a dense cloud.

Helicopters lift off the ground and hover in the air when their rotors force air downward. As long as the helicopter is moving forward, the flowing sand, called "wash," is not a problem. This is because the helicopter stays ahead of the blinding cloud of sand. When a helicopter  lands, however, it is not moving forward and is surrounded by the wash. Pilots landing in the desert learn to land by "feel" since they are not able to see exactly where they are setting down. In addition to checking instruments, the pilot also brings the aircraft down slowly enough that the pilot's own body senses the landing as a gentle bump.

Attack!

One afternoon, Chief Warrant Officer 2 Marc Macaspac was making his routine daily commute from one military base to another when he received an urgent call from work. On that afternoon, an army convoy, or group of military vehicles, had come under attack. One of the US soldiers had been hit, and a rocket-propelled grenade (RPG) had hit a Humvee military vehicle.

This was April 10, 2004, and Macaspac was in Iraq. He was a helicopter pilot who served on a team of two OH-58 Kiowa Warrior helicopters. They live at one base and fly to work at another.

The two Kiowa Warrior helicopters flew to the area where the convoy was. As they arrived, they saw soldiers and civilians running to avoid opposing fire. But the helicopter crews could not tell where the fire was coming from. The Kiowa team used their radios to contact the soldiers on the ground and asked them to mark their positions with red smoke. That way, if the helicopter crews saw

A Kiowa Warrior runs reconnaissance in southern Afghanistan.

rifle fire coming from an area without red smoke, they would know where the opposing fighters were hidden.

As they scouted the area to find out where the opposing fire was coming from, the pilots flew their Kiowas under power lines and between trees. They needed to fly low so that they could spot the fighters but fast enough so that the helicopters wouldn't be hit by the fighters.

As they flew near the convoy, Macaspac saw that the US soldiers were shooting into a line of trees. He and his team flew into the trees to investigate.

Just beyond the edge of the trees, Macaspac spotted a group of about five men crouching in a pit, all dressed in black and holding AK-47 assault rifles. The Kiowa helicopters were no more than 25 feet (7.6 meters) from the men in the pit. Macaspac told his team to keep flying and let the men in the pit think that they had not been spotted. The helicopters flew on for another half mile, then turned back. Macaspac's copilot fired their machine gun, but it jammed. Thinking quickly, Macaspac flew the helicopter up over the trees and fired his M-4 rifle into the pit.

Macaspac's team had rockets, but they were difficult to fire straight down. So Macaspac moved the helicopter directly above, pointed its nose down, and fired the rockets. Meanwhile, the second Kiowa Warrior came up with its machine gun firing. Together, the two helicopters cleared the area. US soldiers soon discovered that the men in the pit had been the only ones firing on the convoy. The battle was over.

Chief Warrant Officer 2 Marc Macaspac and Chief Warrant Officer 2 Eric Bushmaker, the pilot of the second helicopter, received the Air Medal with Valor Device for their heroism and bravery.

How Does a Helicopter Attack?

Attack helicopters are light, two-seat, single-rotor aircraft that are designed to attack ground forces. They are armored and carry weapons and sensors to seek, attack, and destroy targets. Depending on the helicopter, its weapons, and its mission, the targets may include armored vehicles, buildings, troops, ships, or submarines. There are many kinds of attack helicopters. They include the OH-58D Kiowa Warrior and the AH-64 Apache used by the army, the navy's SH-2 Sea Sprite, and the AH-1 Cobra, used by the marines. The coast guard's MH-64A Stingray is an interdiction helicopter. Armed like an attack helicopter, its mission is to stop smugglers and dangerous watercraft.

Attack helicopters usually carry a two-person crew of pilot and copilot. The pilot flies the helicopter. The copilot helps navigate, or direct where they are going, and helps fly the helicopter when

An army AH-64 Apache is an attack helicopter. Here, one takes off from the USS *Ponce.*

needed. The copilot also fills the role of gunner, firing weapons while the pilot keeps the helicopter moving.

Attack helicopters are among the fastest helicopters. The AH-64 Apache can fly as fast as 225 miles per hour (362 kph). Some, such as the Apache, are designed to fly during daylight hours. Others, such as the Kiowa Warrior, are designed mostly for night flight. They carry several types of equipment to help pilots see and navigate in darkness. One such system is a thermal imaging system to help pilots locate targets. These systems sense heat from the ground and convert the heat into pictures. The hotter an object is, the brighter its image.

An aviation electronics technician checks the operating and navigation systems of an HH-60H Sea Hawk helicopter.

An OH-58D Kiowa Warrior, an army scout and reconnaissance aircraft, fires a rocket during a test flight.

Kiowa Warrior Fact Sheet

PRIMARY USE: Attack helicopter
HEIGHT: 12 feet, 10 inches (4 m)
WIDTH: 6 feet, 5 inches (2 m)
LENGTH: 33 feet, 4 inches (10 m)
ROTOR DIAMETER: 35 feet (11 m)
MAXIMUM SPEED: 128 mph (206 kph)
CREW MEMBERS: Pilot, copilot
WEAPONS: Rocket launchers, machine guns, missile launchers

Attack helicopters also carry advanced "visionics." These are electronics systems that help pilots see in all types of weather. Some systems include helmet-mounted displays, which project navigational information on the visor of the pilot's helmet. This includes altitude (how high the helicopter is flying), airspeed, and flight path. This way, the information is right in front of the pilot's eyes. Visionics systems can also find enemy locations and send that information to other aircraft or ground forces.

Attack helicopters are usually equipped with weapons towers. Each tower can include missiles, rockets, or machine guns. The missiles and rockets can pierce the armor on most armored vehicles, such as tanks, at a range of several thousand feet.

Helicopters to the Rescue

The coast guard frequently uses helicopters during its search-and-rescue operations. Employing the Eurocopter HH-65A Dolphin, a twin-engine, single main rotor, a crew of four (pilot, copilot, flight mechanic, and rescue swimmer) is able to make an unaided approach to the water and bring the aircraft into a stable 50-foot (15-m) hover. They can also automatically fly search patterns, which allow the crew to engage in other tasks at the same time. The Dolphin can be deployed from the shore or from a ship. It is also used for drug interdiction, ice breaking, homeland security, and pollution control missions.

A helicopter rescues three people who crashed into the Pacific Ocean during a failed attempt to fly around the earth in a balloon.

CHAPTER 4

Helping the Wounded

Air force Staff Sergeant Kevin Stewart will never forget the night of March 2, 2002. He found himself rushing to the scene of a battle between US soldiers and the Taliban in Afghanistan aboard one of two HH-60G Pave Hawk helicopters. Three of the soldiers had been critically injured in the firefight and needed evacuation and immediate medical attention. The soldiers were supporting Operation Anaconda, with a mission of rooting out the Taliban—a militant Islamist group that had been in power in Afghanistan. The United States was at war with the Taliban because they would not turn over the people who had been responsible for the terrorist attacks on the United States on September 11, 2001.

As the pilot and copilot flew the aircraft, Stewart, the gunner, readied the machine gun in case of trouble. The crew used night vision goggles as they tried to locate the troops. They did not know exactly where they were going. They knew only the general location of the soldiers. The Pave Hawks sped along at just 100 feet (30 m) above the ground, hoping to spot the wounded men before Taliban soldiers found them.

At last Stewart spotted the soldiers and pointed out the area to the pilot. Bullets flew as opposing fighters shot at them. Stewart fired back at the opposing fighters using his helicopter's machine gun as both Pave Hawks landed. Stewart's return fire gave the US soldiers enough time to get the wounded soldiers onto the helicopters.

As they took off, the sky lit up with RPGs and tracer bullets. These are special bullets containing a powder that burns bright

On board a helicopter in Afghanistan, a US Army crew chief helps treat a marine wounded by an improvised explosive device.

Two soldiers help a third onto a US Army medical evacuation helicopter in southern Afghanistan.

red so the gunner can see where the rounds are going. As Stewart fired back, the pilot decided on a quick route out of the area. Within fifteen minutes, they had the wounded men back at a US air base. All three soldiers that they rescued survived.

Later, Stewart said that in the thick of the battle he had not even been aware of the intensity of the opposing fire. His main thought, he said, had been to do his job and ensure that his crew made it home safely.

For his actions that day, Staff Sergeant Kevin Stewart was awarded the Distinguished Flying Cross. He was humble about receiving the award. "This is a great honor," he said. "All the crew deserved this."

What Can the Pave Hawk Carry?

The Pave Hawk and the similar Black Hawk are both light transport helicopters. The Pave Hawk is used by the air force, while the Black Hawk is used by the army. The two helicopters are the same model, but the Pave Hawk has more advanced communications, navigation, and weapons systems. Other transport helicopters include the CH53-D Sea Stallion, used by the navy and marines. The HH-60 Jayhawk, used by the coast guard, is a multipurpose helicopter that is often used for light transport, as well as interdiction and rescue.

A Pave Hawk can transport an eleven-person infantry squadron and all of its equipment. It can move the troops into or out of battle more quickly than ground vehicles can. Small transport helicopters can also carry a Howitzer, a type of cannon, and its six-member crew in a single flight.

Most small transport helicopters carry a crew of four. Roles of the crew members vary. The Pave Hawk's crew, for example, consists of a pilot, copilot, flight engineer, and gunner. The pilot and copilot fly and navigate the helicopter. The flight engineer checks the aircraft before and after a flight and takes care of any small problems during the flight. The gunner controls the weapons and fires back if the helicopter is under attack.

Light transport helicopters are often used in military rescue operations to move wounded soldiers to field hospitals. They may also fly as support during transport or rescue operations. They watch out for and fire at opposing forces while other helicopters land to pick up equipment or soldiers.

Transport helicopters are often used in civilian rescue operations as well. The military may rescue people during natural disasters. Air ambulance companies use small transport helicopters to get injured people from the scene of an accident to a hospital quickly. Often they buy used military helicopters for this purpose.

Helicopters Helping in the Fight Against Disease

During 2014 and 2015, the deadly Ebola virus killed more than eight thousand people in Africa and threatened to spread to other continents. The outbreak crippled countries with already poor health care systems. The epidemic hit the hardest in Liberia, Sierra Leone, and Guinea. In response, the United Nations Mission on Ebola Emergency Response (UNMEER) sent medical and military personnel to Africa to aid in the containment of the disease. UNMEER has focused on logistics and has brought a variety of vehicles to the continent, including helicopters. These choppers provide improved transportation for community mobilization workers to find infected people and stop them from spreading the disease.

Airmen off-load pallets of humanitarian aid from a KC-10 Extender onto a vehicle in Dakar, Senegal. The airmen will then transfer it to a C-130J Super Hercules so it can be flown to Monrovia, Liberia, where an Ebola virus outbreak has devastated the country and others in West Africa.

HH-60 Pave Hawk

PRIMARY USE: Combat and search-and-rescue helicopter
HEIGHT: 16 feet, 8 inches (5 m)
LENGTH: 64 feet, 8 inches (20 m)
ROTOR DIAMETER: 53 feet, 7 inches (16 m)
MAXIMUM SPEED: 184 mph (296 kph)
CREW: Pilot, copilot, flight engineer, gunner
WEAPONS: Two machine guns

A US Air Force HH-60 Pave Hawk helicopter, meant for combat search and rescue, lands at Bagram Air Field in Afghanistan.

CHAPTER 5

Hauling Heavy Loads

They were sinking and running out of time. Trapped in the quicksand when their Humvee drove off the road during Operation Desert Storm in 1991, the army lieutenants knew their vehicle would eventually be buried. They radioed for help, but it was going to be several days before anyone could come to their rescue. A crane could have pulled the Humvee and its crew free, but there were no cranes available. The only other way to free them was with a CH-47 Chinook helicopter.

By the time the Chinook's pilot, Chief Warrant Officer Glenn Bloom, and a crew chief arrived in their helicopter, the Humvee had sunk up to its windows in the quicksand. Bloom landed the Chinook in the quicksand but kept the rotor spinning. This kept most of the weight of the helicopter off the quicksand and prevented the Chinook from rolling over and sinking as the Humvee had. Only the helicopter's wheels sank into the sand.

The crew chief jumped out of the helicopter with a sling held over his head. Though he quickly sank chest-deep into the sand, he worked his way over to attach the sling to the Humvee. It was hard work, and the operation took more than thirty minutes. At last the crew chief gave the signal that the Humvee was ready to be lifted from the sand.

But first Bloom had to lift the Chinook out of the quicksand. He carefully rocked the helicopter back and forth until he was able to pull out all of its wheels. Next, Bloom flew the Chinook over the top of the Humvee. The crew chief connected the helicopter's hook to the sling attached to the Humvee. Then, with the helicopter, Bloom lifted the Humvee out of the quicksand and set it down on the road. The Humvee weighed 5,200 pounds (2,359 kilograms)—almost three tons, or about the same as one and a half cars!

Bloom gave the grateful Humvee crew some food, picked up his crew chief, and flew back to base. The powerful Chinook had stepped outside of its usual role as a transport helicopter to take on a successful rescue mission.

What Can the Chinook Carry?

The Chinook is a heavy transport helicopter, used by the army for carrying equipment, food, weapons, and troops. Though reporters sometimes describe it as slow and clumsy, the Chinook is actually very agile and capable of flying 184 mph (296 kph), as fast as some attack helicopters. Other heavy transport helicopters include the CH-46 Sea Knight and the CH53-E Super Stallion, used by the navy and marines.

The Chinook is the helicopter that the army relies on in its operations in Afghanistan. The average elevation, or height, of the Hindu Kush Mountains, which cover most of Afghanistan, is almost 9,000 feet (2,743 m). The air at this elevation is thin. Helicopters with only a single horizontal rotor do not have enough air to push down and lift off the ground. Only the Chinook with its double rotors has enough power to lift in the thin atmosphere.

In preparation of returning home to the United States after nine months in Afghanistan, soldiers load CH-47 helicopters onto a C-5 Galaxy.

Heavy transport helicopters are large-bodied aircraft. The cabin of a Chinook, for example, holds forty-two cubic meters of cargo in an area of twenty-one square meters, a space large enough to hold two full-sized military Humvees. It has seating for thirty-three combat troops plus three crew members. In an emergency, up to twice as many troops can be carried, with some sitting on the floor in the aisles.

Since heavy transport helicopters are not generally used as attack aircraft, the weapons they carry are mostly for defense. They are usually armed with machine guns. They may also carry a missile approach warner, which lets the pilot know that a missile

US Marines fly a CH-53E Super Stallion helicopter during a sling load operation.

is approaching. A radar warner tells the pilot that opposing forces are tracking the helicopter with radar and may be about to launch an attack. A jammer sends strong electronic signals to confuse the radar of opposing forces, making it harder for them to launch an attack.

Transport helicopters may also carry chaff and flare dispensers. These systems eject small pieces of metal foil, or chaff, as well as flares (flammable wands that can be ignited to give off light) from the helicopter. The chaff and flares attract radar-guided or heat-seeking missiles so the weapons will explode harmlessly in the air, away from the helicopter. Chaff is also another way to confuse opposing radar.

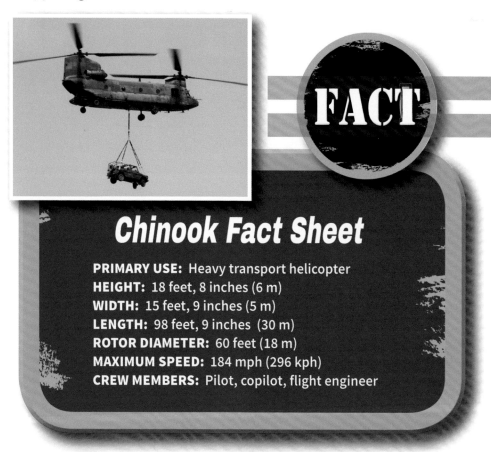

FACT

Chinook Fact Sheet

PRIMARY USE: Heavy transport helicopter
HEIGHT: 18 feet, 8 inches (6 m)
WIDTH: 15 feet, 9 inches (5 m)
LENGTH: 98 feet, 9 inches (30 m)
ROTOR DIAMETER: 60 feet (18 m)
MAXIMUM SPEED: 184 mph (296 kph)
CREW MEMBERS: Pilot, copilot, flight engineer

Sling Loading

Sling loading is a method for a transport helicopter to carry cargo outside of its cabin. Beneath the helicopter are three hooks. One is forward, or at the front of the helicopter, one is in the center, and one is aft, or at the rear.

The forward and aft hooks can carry loads of 17,000 pounds (7,711 kg) each. The center hook alone can carry loads as heavy as 26,000 pounds (11,793 kg). That is similar to the weight of two medium-sized African elephants! The Chinook is so powerful that it can sling load and carry another 25,000-pound (11,340-kg) Chinook helicopter.

A CH-53E Super Stallion transports an army CH-47 Chinook in Afghanistan.

CHAPTER 6

So You Want to Become a Military Helicopter Pilot?

Selection and training to become a military helicopter pilot take hard work, practice, and dedication. While most programs require students to complete officer training before entering the flight program, the air force includes training for students who have not yet completed officer training.

Each program differs in its details, but they all share a similar format. For example, aviator training for the navy and coast guard takes place at naval air stations in Florida, Mississippi, and Texas. Air force bases in Texas, Oklahoma, and Georgia conduct joint training for air force and naval pilots. The army has a flight school in Alabama. Later, when students choose to specialize as helicopter pilots, those in the navy, marines, and coast guard will train together at a base in Florida.

Phase 1: Pre-flight Training

Phase 1 includes academic classes and pre-flight training. Before students get their hands on the controls of an aircraft, they must know how aircraft work. Students spend about six weeks in intense study, learning about engineering, aerodynamics (the forces that allow an aircraft to fly), navigation instruments (which help pilots find their way in the air), various aircraft systems, and survival skills. When they are not in front of a computer, working hard at computer-based lessons, students practice simulated parachute jumps from towers.

Phase 2: Flight Training

Phase 2, which lasts about twenty-two weeks (just under six months) is flight training. Regardless of what kind of aircraft the student pilots want to fly later, they all begin with computer-based flight simulators. After that, they actually fly for the first time, in a small airplane known as a trainer. With an instructor in the seat beside them, students learn the basics first: how to take off, fly,

Army paratroopers prepare to jump from a UH-60M Black Hawk helicopter.

A pilot checks a navigational chart while flying an MH-53E Sea Dragon helicopter.

and land safely. They practice "touch-and-go" landings, where they touch the wheels of their airplane to the runway and take right off again. This skill comes in handy in combat situations, where a pilot might attempt a landing but suddenly comes under attack and is forced to take off again.

After they master the basics, students learn some simple aerobatics, such as barrel rolls (rolling the aircraft in midair), and they learn to fly solo. They also learn to use the aircraft's instruments to help them navigate. Then students learn to fly in formation with other planes and how to fly safely at low altitudes.

At the end of Phase 2, students decide what kind of pilot they would like to be. The choices include fighter or bomber pilot, tanker or airlift pilot, or helicopter pilot. Fighter planes attack other planes, as well as ground targets. Bombers drop bombs or missiles on ground targets. Tanker planes carry fuel for other aircraft. Airlift planes carry cargo and personnel.

Students may not always get the "track" they request. Those who earned the best scores on written and in-flight tests during their training often get their first pick. Each track can take a certain number of students. If a track fills up, other students who wanted that track may have to choose another.

Phase 3: Advanced Aircraft Training

In the final phase, students learn to fly the aircraft that they will specialize in. They usually attend a school that specializes in a certain kind of aircraft. For helicopter pilots, the program involves about twenty-eight weeks of intensive training in flying helicopters.

Since helicopters work differently from airplanes, taking off, landing, and flying them require a new set of skills. Students learn to use a helicopter's controls and instruments. They practice night flying and low-level flight. Graduates may then receive special training in a specific type of helicopter before they are finally assigned to a military unit as a pilot.

Careers in Helicopters Outside of the Military

Once a helicopter pilot leaves the military there are many opportunities to continue flying helicopters.

Law enforcement is one career option for a military helicopter pilot. Police forces often need helicopters to watch busy freeways and spot accidents and reckless drivers. Pilots may watch from the air when police on the ground move in to stop a crime, and follow any escaping suspects.

Air ambulance services need experienced pilots who can respond to emergencies. They may be called on to rescue injured people from the scene of a traffic accident or from remote wilderness areas. Air ambulance pilots often have to fly in bad weather and in other dangerous conditions that military pilots have experienced.

Even Hollywood needs helicopter pilots. Movie studios often need them to make aerial photo flights in the filming of movies. They also need stunt pilots, who carry out dangerous stunts for action movies.

Missions of Medical Evacuation

The term "medevac" is short for "medical evacuation." It refers to an airplane or helicopter used as an ambulance. Helicopters are more commonly used because of their ability to easily take off from the scene of an accident and land in a relatively small space, such as the roof of a hospital.

Sometimes medevacs are called air ambulances. When people are seriously injured in traffic accidents, for example, they are often airlifted to nearby trauma centers (hospitals that specialize in medical emergencies), where teams of doctors can work to save their lives. A medevac can get a person to a hospital far faster than an ambulance on the ground.

Medevacs were first developed during the Korean War (1950–1953) to help save soldiers' lives. The TV show *M*A*S*H*, popular in the 1970s, was based on the experiences of army surgeons and demonstrated how helicopters were used. The show was set during the Korean War. The name MASH stands for Mobile Army Surgical Hospital.

Polish soldiers and a US Army medical team evacuate a wounded Iraqi soldier.

With the danger of combat behind them, former military helicopter pilots have the skills to succeed in any helicopter-related career. Most military helicopter pilots know how to operate their aircraft in difficult and dangerous conditions where lives and expensive equipment are at stake, and they know how to handle pressure. Useful in any career, whether involving helicopters or not, this knowledge stays with a pilot long after he or she leaves the military.

Do You Have What It Takes?

If you are a person who does not give up easily, you have one of the most important qualities of a successful military pilot. A military helicopter pilot also has to be physically fit. Becoming physically fit and staying fit is a lifelong pursuit and can begin today. Pilots also have positive attitudes. They are "can-do" people. They must be resourceful and find ways to solve problems under stressful conditions.

Pilots in the military must also love adventure. There is no doubt that flying a helicopter in a war zone is thrilling, but there are responsibilities every pilot must face. Each mission must be completed to the best of the pilot's ability because other people's lives depend upon it.

1916—First helicopter is flown by Raúl Pateras de Pescara of Argentina.

1939—Russian Igor Sikorsky, known as the "father of helicopters," builds the VS-300.

1943—Sikorsky's R-4 helicopter model is put into production for military use in World War II.

1950–1953—Helicopters are used in the Korean War to transport wounded soldiers to field hospitals.

1965–1973—Helicopters are used extensively during the Vietnam War for medical evacuation, as well as attack.

2007—The first tiltrotor helicopter, the V-22 Osprey, is introduced into military operations.

US Marine Corps Osprey Tiltrotor

Air Medal—Military decoration awarded for meritorious achievement while participating in aerial flight.

copilot—The second pilot in an aircraft, who assists the pilot and may take over if the pilot is injured.

crew chief—Helicopter crew member who takes care of and repairs the aircraft.

flight engineer—Helicopter crew member who inspects the helicopter before and after a flight and helps take care of it during a flight.

interdiction—Stopping the opposing side, such as smugglers or dangerous watercraft.

lift—The force that holds a helicopter or other aircraft in the air. It is caused by a downward flow of air off a helicopter's rotor or an airplane's wing.

machine gun—An automatic weapon that can fire many bullets rapidly.

medevac—Medical evacuation.

missile—A rocket carrying explosive ammunition that may be launched by remote control.

navigate—To guide an aircraft along a planned route.

pilot—Helicopter crew member in charge of flying the aircraft.

radar—Tool that detects objects by sending out radio waves that bounce off of the objects.

rocket—An explosive weapon that is propelled by an engine.

rocket-propelled grenade (RPG)—A small rocket fired from a shoulder-mounted launcher, used against aircraft and tanks.

rotor— A set of blades on a helicopter that turn, producing the airflow that moves the aircraft forward and helps lift it into the air.

tiltrotor—An aircraft that combines the vertical lift capability of a helicopter with the speed and range of a fixed-wing aircraft.

visionics—Electrical systems on a helicopter that enhance what a pilot is able to see in various conditions.

BOOKS

Bowden, Mark. *Black Hawk Down.* New York: Grove Press, 2010.

Crosby, Francis. *The World Encyclopedia of Military Helicopters.* London: Lorenz Books, 2013.

Owen, Mark, and Kevin Maurer. *No Easy Day.* New York: NAL Trade, 2014.

Whittle, Richard. *The Dream Machine.* New York: Simon and Schuster, 2011.

Wyckoff, Edwin Brit. *Helicopter Man: Igor Sikorsky and His Amazing Invention.* Berkeley Heights, N.J.: Enslow Publishers, Inc., 2010.

WEB SITES

army.mil
Learn more about the US Army.

navy.mil
Discover what it takes to join the US Navy.

uscg.mil
Read about the US Coast Guard.

usmc.mil
Visit the US Marine Corps Web site.

sikorskyarchives.com
Explore the life and career of Igor Sikorsky.

Sikorsky S-55 UH-19D Chickasaw

INDEX